SEARCHING FOR

UFOs, ALIENS,
AND
MEN IN BLACK

BY MICHAEL BURGAN

Consultant:
Dr. Andrew Nichols
Director of the
American Institute of Parapsychology
Thomasville, Georgia

CAPSTONE PRESS
a capstone imprint

Velocity is published by Capstone Press,
1710 Roe Crest Drive, North Mankato, Minnesota 56003.
www.capstonepub.com

Library of Congress Cataloging-in-Publication Data
Burgan, Michael.
  Searching for aliens, UFOs, and men in black / by Michael Burgan.
      p. cm.—(Velocity. Unexplained phenomena)
  Includes bibliographical references and index.
  Summary: "Covers UFOs, aliens, and alien abductions, including specific examples and skeptical
arguments against the belief in aliens"—Provided by publisher.
  ISBN 978-1-4296-4816-5 (library binding)
  1. Unidentified flying objects—Juvenile literature. 2. Men in black (UFO phenomenon)—Juvenile
literature. 3. Extraterrestrial beings—Juvenile literature. I. Title. II. Series.
  TL789.2.B86 2011
  001.942—dc22   2010036928

Editorial Credits
Mandy Robbins, editor; Matt Bruning, designer; Marcie Spence, media researcher;
    Laura Manthe, production specialist

Photo Credits
Capstone Studio: Karon Dubke, 16 (scalpel and scissors), 36-37; Don Berliner, 23 (inset); Getty
Images Inc.: Carl Iwasaki/Time Life Pictures, 28; Mary Evans Picture Library: 12-13, 24 (left), 30
(bottom), 32-33, 34-35, 40 (top); Newscom: Columbia Pictures, 41 (bottom); Shutterstock: 06photo,
29 (bottom), akud, 21 (middle), Alex James Bramwell, 31 (bottom), Andrea Danti, 22-23, Andresr,
cover (man), ArchMan, 25 (top), 43 (top), Arena Creative, 38 (top), B & T Media Group Inc.,
26 (hawk), bocky, 14 (clouds), Brent Walker, 14 (flames), broukoid, cover (ufos), 5 (ufo), 19, 29
(middle), Bruce Rolff, 42 (top), Christopher Poliquin, 41 (top), clearviewstock, cover (stars), (design
elements), cs333, 20 (bottom), Danylchenko Iaroslav, 31 (middle), Dmitry Bodrov, 5 (top left),
Dr_Flash, (design element), ducu59us, 24 (bottom right), Dudarev Mikhail, 6-7 (pyramids), Eduard
Harkonen, 17 (bottom), ELEN, 26-27, Elena Elisseeva, 4 (bottom), Fedorov Oleksiy, 25 (bottom),
Giovanni Benintende, 8-9 (sky), Gl0ck, 9 (top left), 39 (bottom), happydancing, 5 (sky), ilFede, 29
(top), Ilja Masik, 7 (top), 26 (plane), James Steidl, 8 (telescope), Jason Stitt, 9 (middle), javarman, 7
(middle), Kenneth V. Pilon, 20 (middle), Kevin Bassie, cover (fence), Kevotech, 30 (top), kickstand,
4 (top), Kitch Bain, 42 (bottom), koya979, 21 (bottom), kropic1, (design element), Leelaryonkul, 5
(top right), Matthew Jacques, 17 (top), Michelangelus, 10 (rocket), 14 (UFO), Mona Makela, (design
element), mozzyb, 44-45, Nailia Schwarz, 9 (top right), Nataliia Natykach, 7 (bottom), New Image, 9
(bottom), Noel Powell, Schaumburg, 42-43 (background), Peter Baxter, (design element), photoBeard,
16 (bottom), Picsfive, 21 (top), Robyn Mackenzie, 24 (ID tag), Roman Krochuk, cover (green lights),
Samot, 20 (top), sgame, 37 (top), Shalygin, 10-11 (sky), Shiva, cover (alien), sn4ke, 39 (top), takito, 41
(film frames), Tatiana Popova, 31 (top), Ton Lammerts, 26 (hot air balloon), Valentin Agapov, 18-19,
40 (bottom), W. Scott, 15, Witold Kaszkin, 39 (middle)

Printed in the United States of America in North Mankato, Minnesota.
042013
007252R

TABLE OF CONTENTS

A BRIGHT LIGHT
IN THE NIGHT

A bright light darts across the night sky. The light stops for a moment before speeding off. No airplane moves like that. What could it be?

The light might be a secret government aircraft. Or maybe it's a meteor. But until scientists can explain it, the light is an unidentified flying object (UFO).

People around the world report seeing things in the sky they cannot explain. In some cases, scientists or government officials question these people. In most cases, the UFO becomes an IFO—an identified flying object.

Experts study to see if aircraft or natural objects, such as planets, can explain UFO sightings.

Even a flock of birds can trick people into thinking they have seen something mysterious.

But scientists cannot always say what a UFO is. Some **ufologists** believe spacecraft from other planets account for some UFO sightings. Are aliens visiting Earth? Have some landed here? Examine the evidence and decide for yourself.

ufologist — a person who studies and tries to explain UFOs

CHAPTER 1

UFOs IN HISTORY

Some researchers think people have been seeing UFOs for thousands of years. Ancient writers reported seeing bright lights or fires in the sky. These people had little knowledge about the stars and planets. Many UFO sightings in ancient times could probably be explained by modern science. Still, some people firmly believe that ancient people made contact with aliens.

ADVANCED BUILDING STRUCTURES

One argument for alien contact in ancient times focuses on large ancient structures. Structures like the pyramids in Egypt baffle scientists. They were built with huge stone blocks. These blocks would have been difficult for modern machines to handle. How could ancient people move them with only simple tools? To some people, the only possible answer is that the Egyptians had help. Advanced beings from outer space must have brought their technology to Earth.

FACT

The Egyptian pyramids were built between 4,000 and 5,000 years ago. The Egyptians hadn't even begun using wheels at that time.

FLYING ARTIFACTS

Believers in aliens also point to certain **artifacts** to support their belief. Artifacts from ancient graves in Egypt and Columbia resemble jet airplanes. Some people believe ancient people learned flight technology from aliens.

DETAILED MAPS

Some people believe that very accurate ancient maps support a belief in aliens. They say that these maps couldn't be so accurate without flight technology. They think this technology must have come from aliens.

BIBLE STORIES

Some people believe that stories in the Bible point to alien activity. Could stories of flying chariots and angels really be about beings from outer space?

artifact	an object used in the past that was made by people

ENTERING THE AGE OF REASON

By the 1600s, modern science was developing. Scientists tried to explain **supernatural** events with their new knowledge. In 1608 Hans Lippershey invented the first telescope. Soon astronomers learned that comets and meteors explained most of the ancient UFO sightings.

supernatural	describes something that cannot be given an ordinary explanation

1890s AIRSHIPS

Even though science explained most UFOs, some people continued to see strange things in the sky. In the late 1890s, hundreds of North Americans spotted UFOs.

The first sightings were reported in California. Eventually, UFOs were spotted in Washington, Nevada, Texas, Nebraska, and other states. The flying objects could not have been airplanes. By this time, humans had learned to fly using hot air balloons. But airplanes were not invented until several years later.

Some people said they saw a light first, then the aircraft.

Some witnesses claimed the objects had wings and propellers.

In some of the reports, people said they saw humans on board the UFOs. They heard the crew on the aircraft speaking English.

Some of the 1890s sightings were actually planets or other objects that naturally appear in the sky. Other sightings were pranks. Tricksters had tied lights to kites and sent them into the sky at night. However, some of the sightings remained unexplained.

FOO FIGHTERS

During World War II (1939-1945), U.S. and European military pilots reported strange lights and objects around their planes. American pilots called them "foo fighters." In some cases, the UFOs seemed to follow the planes. Some people thought they were devices created by the Germans to interfere with enemy radar. Some scientists assumed that the lights were an illusion caused by electricity. Others thought they were reflections of sunlight off tiny pieces of ice high in the sky.

illusion	something that appears to be real but isn't

GHOST ROCKETS

During World War II, Germany developed the world's first rockets and jet planes. Humans and weapons could travel faster than ever before.

After the war, people across Europe and the United States said they saw rocket-shaped aircraft in the sky. The aircraft traveled at high speeds and could quickly change direction. These UFOs were soon called "ghost rockets."

A scientist who got a closer view of one of the craft said it was 90 feet (27 meters) long and made of metal.

One pilot saw an aircraft fall as a meteor would. But then the UFO quickly rose up again—something a meteor could not do.

Some witnesses said ghost rockets had blue and green smoke that trailed from their tails.

After the war, the United States and the Soviet Union were enemies. U.S. officials worried that the Soviets had captured German rockets and built their own. The U.S. government suspected that's what the ghost rockets were.

Many ghost rocket sightings came from Sweden, which is near the Soviet Union. U.S. and British officials convinced the Swedes to study reports of the ghost rockets. The Swedes found pieces of metal that they thought came from crashed ghost rockets. They couldn't tell if the metal came from a rocket or a missile. The Swedes finally concluded that they found no proof of a secret Soviet missile test. No one knows what these mysterious objects were.

FACT

In 1946 the Norwegian government asked local newspapers to stop writing about the ghost rockets. The government feared people would worry about a possible enemy attack.

FLYING SAUCERS

Around 3:00 p.m. on June 24, 1947, Kenneth Arnold flew his small plane near Washington's Mount Rainier. Suddenly, he saw a flash in the sky—then another. He noticed a series of bright lights in the distance. At first he thought they were jets. But the objects didn't look or fly like any plane he had ever seen.

Arnold later reported that he had seen nine crescent-shaped objects. He compared the way they moved to saucers skipping across water. Soon newspapers were reporting his sighting of "flying saucers."

The Arnold sighting made the term "flying saucer" popular. But it was not the first time the term had been used to describe a UFO. In 1878 a Texas farmer reported seeing a large flying saucer.

WHAT WAS IT?

Arnold thought he might have seen a secret U.S. government aircraft. U.S. officials denied this. Over the years, scientists developed other explanations for what Arnold saw. One said it was a **mirage**. Another thought Arnold might have seen snow blowing off the mountains. No official explanation was ever made.

mirage	something that appears to be there but is not; mirages are often caused by light rays bending where air layers of different temperatures meet

CHAPTER 2

UFOs AND THE AIR FORCE

CRASH AT ROSWELL!

Soon after the Arnold sighting, another UFO story made news. On the evening of July 4, 1947, there was a thunderstorm over Corona, New Mexico. During the storm, rancher William "Mac" Brazel heard a loud noise like an explosion. The next day he rode his horse around the ranch. Brazel found a large **debris** field of metallic material. It looked like some kind of aircraft had crashed there. On July 6, 1947, Brazel drove to nearby Roswell to report his discovery to authorities.

Army Air Force officials at the local military base investigated the site. On July 8, they issued a press release. It said the debris was the wreckage of a flying disc.

debris	scattered pieces of something that has been broken or destroyed

JUST A WEATHER BALLOON?

The next day, however, the military had a new story. The wreckage was not a flying saucer. It was a rubber weather balloon. Attached to it was a foil radar and a wooden target. The target helped radar stations track the balloon. The military used it to study the speed and direction of winds.

Most people believed the new version of the story. But many people who had seen the wreckage did not. They claimed the materials Brazel found were not simple rubber, foil, and wood. Brazel told a newspaper reporter that he had found weather balloons before. This wreckage didn't look like any weather balloon he'd ever seen.

ROSWELL CITY LIMITS ELEV. 3570

FACT

In the 1990s, the U.S. government changed its story again. Officials claimed the debris was from a top-secret balloon called Project Mogul. The project was an attempt to detect Soviet bombs.

WAS IT A COVER UP?

In the 1970s, ufologists began taking another look at the Roswell incident. They questioned citizens and military officials who had lived and worked there in 1947. Some people claimed that wreckage had been found at more than one place near Roswell.

A few people said bodies of aliens had been discovered in the wreckage. They claimed the bodies were secretly taken to a military base in Ohio. Some people even reported that one of the aliens survived the crash. This photo shows a re-creation of what these aliens may have looked like.

They had large heads and big eyes.

The aliens were described as similar to humans in some ways. But they were obviously not human. The bodies were the size of a 10-year-old child.

Some people said the aliens had two holes in their heads where a nose would be.

A WITNESS SPEAKS

In 2006 a former member of the U.S. Air Force came forward with a story about the Roswell crash. The man went by the false name Eli Benjamin to protect his identity. Benjamin said he saw the aliens from the Roswell crash. He said they had gray skin and no hair. He also noted an awful smell in the area.

Military officials told Benjamin that something terrible would happen to his family if he revealed what he saw. He waited almost 40 years before breaking his silence.

TOP SECRET

PRIVATE

The military claimed the "aliens" were just crash test dummies. The dummies had been used in impact tests.

What really happened at Roswell in 1947? Did aliens crash there? Was the U.S. government testing a top-secret aircraft? Many people accept the government's story. Others are convinced that the government is covering up the truth.

MYSTERY IN RENDLESHAM FOREST

Great Britain

Rendlesham Forest ▼

Rendlesham Forest is located near two U.S. Air Force bases in Great Britain. On a December evening in 1980, several airmen reported seeing odd lights in the forest. Men from one base said they saw a triangle-shaped metal object. It seemed to have three legs. Later, one person also claimed to have seen aliens in the woods.

FACT

The strange events in Rendlesham Forest earned it the nickname "England's Roswell."

THE HALT INVESTIGATION

After the strange reports, Lieutenant Colonel Charles Halt took a team to investigate. The investigators saw three holes in the ground where the UFO had been spotted. The marks formed a triangle. Investigators also found damage to trees in the area. They claimed to have measured high levels of **radiation** as well.

radiation	tiny particles sent out from harmful radioactive material

While Halt and his team were investigating, they saw a bright oval object moving quickly through the forest. Suddenly, the object broke into multiple lights. The lights darted through the sky. Halt's team also reported laser beams shining down from the sky.

Halt made an audio recording of the events as they happened. He later described what he saw in a letter to the British government and the U.S. Air Force. Halt wasn't sure what his team saw. But he believed it was under intelligent control.

FINDING RATIONAL EXPLANATIONS

Scientists and officials from Great Britain and the United States studied the reports from the Rendlesham incident. They had other explanations for the "evidence" at the scene of the crash. They also had possible explanations for what the witnesses said they saw.

The bright lights were from a nearby lighthouse. The lighthouse is about 5 miles (8 kilometers) from the site of the reported UFO. Investigators found that as the light revolves, it appears to flash through the trees.

A meteor shower had occurred on the night of the Halt investigation. Perhaps Halt and his men had confused it for a UFO.

The three holes in the ground also had a logical explanation. Locals recognized them as rabbit burrows.

The damage to the trees was done by forest rangers. The rangers had made small chops in the trees to indicate that they were to be cut down.

The radiation measurements were not actually high for the area. Experts said the forest had normal levels of radiation.

The official reports by both the U.S. and British governments were clear. All of the evidence was explained by natural causes. A spaceship had not landed in Rendlesham Forest.

OFFICIAL

CHAPTER 3

GOVERNMENT STUDIES

PROJECT · SIGN

Throughout 1948 U.S. pilots and scientists reported UFOs. Most military leaders thought the objects were secret Soviet technology. They thought studying UFOs was important to keep the United States safe from an enemy attack. The Air Force created Project Sign for that job.

After months of study, some Project Sign members made a startling suggestion. Some of the UFOs were real objects. But they were not made by humans. One Project Sign report said about 20 percent of UFO sightings could not be explained.

PROJECT·GRUDGE

In 1949 Project Sign became Project Grudge. A general involved in the project concluded that all of the sightings could be explained. Those that were not real aircraft were caused by natural events, illusions, and hoaxes. The government soon cut the staff of Project Grudge. By 1951 only one person was working on the project. Some people think the government did this to hide the presence of aliens from the public.

FACT

Many people believe the name change from Project Sign to Project Grudge was significant. They believe it showed the government's grudge against studying the possibility of alien existence.

In March 1952, Project Grudge was renamed Project Blue Book. The head of the project, Captain Edward J. Ruppelt, wanted to increase efforts to study UFOs. These included filming and audio recording in UFO hot spots. Ruppelt's ideas were rejected. But Blue Book officials did order all Air Force bases to immediately report any UFO sightings.

Captain Ruppelt was head of Project Blue Book until 1953. In 1956 he published a book about what he'd learned about UFOs. Ruppelt's book gave only the facts. The readers could draw their own conclusions.

↗ CAPTAIN EDWARD J. RUPPELT

TOP SECRET

FACT

From June to October of 1952, Project Blue Book received about 1,000 UFO reports. This was more than the government had received during the previous five years.

UFOs AND INVERSION

During July 1952, several radar stations around Washington, D.C. detected many UFOs. The Air Force said a weather event called inversion created the sightings.

During an inversion, a layer of warm air sits above cooler air closer to Earth. This can make radar detect items on the ground instead of in the sky. However, several radar operators who saw the Washington, D.C. UFOs disagreed with this idea. They said the images they saw didn't look like images caused by inversion.

OFFICIAL BLUE BOOK REPORT

In 1955 the U.S. government released a report from Project Blue Book. It said that none of the UFOs studied by Project Blue Book were alien spacecraft. Years later several scientists studied the report. The scientists found many sightings from reliable sources that had not been explained.

THE DURANT REPORT

The United States Central Intelligence Agency (CIA) was also interested in UFOs. In 1953 the CIA hired a group of scientists to study information about UFOs. The group was called the Robertson Panel. The Robertson Panel published its findings in the Durant Report. This report was named after Frederick Durant, a member of the group. The scientists said that a person making a claim about alien existence must have physical proof. Without a spaceship or alien body, there was no proof.

EXPLAINING UFOs

Between 1947 and 1956, 15 to 20 percent of UFO sightings were unexplained by government groups.

80%

15-20%

Most UFO sightings could be explained. Some people had seen balloons, airplanes, birds, or meteors.

A DIFFERENT PERSPECTIVE

Major Dewey J. Fournet disagreed with the Durant Report. He had studied many Project Blue Book reports. Fournet told the Robertson Panel that not all of the sightings could be explained. He believed that when all logical explanations failed, a UFO must have alien origins.

THE CONDON REPORT

The government made its last major report on UFOs in 1969. A group of scientists was hired to study all past UFO reports. Scientist Edward U. Condon led the group. The Condon Report concluded that past years of study had not led to any useful scientific knowledge. The report also said scientists had no proof that aliens had ever visited Earth. The Condon Report did say aliens might exist. But the scientists believed they would not be able to reach Earth for at least 10,000 years.

↗

EDWARD U. CONDON

Because of the Condon Report's findings, the U.S. government officially stopped studying UFOs. Project Blue Book was closed down. The private study of UFOs picked up as the U.S. government stopped its research.

THE CONDON REPORT CAUSES CONTROVERSY

Even though Project Blue Book had ended, pilots continued seeing UFOs in the sky. Pilots were ordered to report UFOs to the Air Force. Some people saw this as evidence of a government cover-up. They wondered why pilots had to report sightings if no one was studying them.

Researchers also learned in 1979 that not all sightings were listed in public files. That meant the scientists working on the Condon Report didn't study all the sightings.

CHAPTER 4

ALIEN CONTACT?

Stories of UFOs are not the only out-of-this-world **controversy**. People have been reporting alien contact as well. Some stories are more incredible than others.

GEORGE ADAMSKI

In 1952 George Adamski reported meeting an alien in the California desert. Adamski said the being had come from Venus. It wanted to tell humans to stop building powerful new bombs. Adamski released photos that he said showed alien spacecraft. He later admitted they were fakes. Adamski also claimed to have made contact with more aliens from other planets.

UFO skeptics ignored Adamski. Ufologists did not believe him either. They thought his tales led people to make fun of the serious study of UFOs.

Flying Saucers Have Landed

Desmond Leslie & George Adamski

In 1953 Adamski published a book titled *Flying Saucers Have Landed*. In the book he claimed to have had contact with aliens he called Venusian Martians.

controversy	something that people disagree about

Even though most people didn't believe Adamski's experiences, more contactees stepped forward. The general public thought these people were lying. University of Wyoming professor Leo Sprinkle did not. He claimed to have seen a flying saucer in 1949. Sprinkle was fascinated by the subject. He began to investigate the experiences of others.

In 1980 a group of UFO contactees began meeting yearly in Colorado. Sprinkle questioned them about their experiences. He found that UFO contactees shared common characteristics.

Contactees were highly intelligent. They preferred to think for themselves rather than following orders.

Contactees reported missing periods of time. They had no idea what happened during these time gaps.

Contactees reported having restless sleep after their encounters. They also had strange dreams.

FACT

Some contactees claim to receive messages from aliens without actually seeing them. They say aliens send thoughts directly into their minds.

ABDUCTION

Betty and Barney Hill reported one of the most incredible UFO stories ever. On September 19, 1961, the Hills were driving from Canada to their New Hampshire home. As they were driving, they saw a strange light in the sky. Eventually, the Hills stopped their car. Barney got out to get a better look at the light. The light approached him. Barney saw that it was actually an aircraft. As it came closer, Barney thought he saw beings inside. He became afraid that the beings would capture him. Barney ran back to the car, and the Hills drove off.

FACT

r their odd
n Hills claimed
es stopped ticking.

MISSING TIME

The Hills claimed
to have left the scene
frantically. After driving
a short time, they realized
they were 30 miles (48 km)
farther down the road than
they thought they should be.
But after arriving home, they
realized their trip had taken two
hours longer than it should have.
Neither Barney nor Betty could
account for the missing time.

THE OFFICIAL REPORT

On September 22, the Hills contacted the local
Air Force base to report their story. The military said
that a UFO had appeared on their radar that evening
as well. Major Paul W. Henderson wrote a report
about the Hills' encounter. He sent it to Project Blue
Book. Project Blue Book explained away both the
Hills' sighting and the object on radar. They blamed
inversion for the faulty radar reading and the light that
the Hills saw in the sky.

AFTER THE ENCOUNTER

After their 1961 experience, the Hills had
more odd experiences. Betty noticed that the
dress she'd been wearing that night was torn.
Barney's shoes had been ruined as well.
Neither could recall how this happened.
And soon Betty began having
nightmares about being taken
aboard an alien spacecraft.
In 1963 the Hills underwent
hypnosis. They hoped it would help
them remember the two hours of
missing time. While they were
hypnotized, both described being
taken aboard an alien spacecraft.
They remembered medical tests
being performed on them. Betty
said that she asked the beings
where they were from. They
showed her a star map.

hypnosis	putting people in a trancelike state to help them remember things

Betty Hill drew the map that she claimed the aliens showed her. It was a fairly accurate drawing of a section of our galaxy.

SCIENTIFIC DEBATE

Since the Hills told their story, hundreds more people have described being kidnapped by aliens. In 1992 scientists met at the Massachusetts Institute of Technology to discuss reported abductions. Strong opinions arose on both sides of the topic. Scientist Don C. Donderi believed the claims of alien abductions could be real. But he admitted there was no proof. Skeptic Philip Klass believed people who reported abductions just wanted attention.

MEN IN BLACK

Some people who reported UFOs said they were visited by mysterious men dressed in black. Many people thought they were government officials. These men questioned them about the sightings.

In 1952 Albert Bender formed the International Flying Saucer Bureau. The organization lasted only a year before Bender shut it down. He later claimed that three men in black suits had visited him. The men threatened Bender's life. They told him to stop saying that UFOs were alien spacecraft. Bender's tale made "men in black" a popular part of many UFO stories. People who believed Bender thought the government was trying to hide what it knew about aliens.

Bender later said that the men who threatened him were not government officials. They were aliens. Bender's story now seemed too strange for most people to believe. But the stories of men in black did not stop with Bender.

FACT

Legends hundreds of years old describe mysterious men dressed in black who visit people. In most of these legends, the men work for the devil.

DEMONS OR ANGELS?

UFO researcher John Keel claimed men in black often knew all the details of UFO sightings. They had this knowledge even though the viewers had never discussed the sightings. Keel believed that these beings could be angels or demons.

PRANKSTERS?

In 1967 the Air Force said that men in black were ordinary humans playing tricks on people. They lied to make people think they worked for the government.

CHAPTER 5

STUDYING UFOs

Governments around the world have studied UFOs that appeared over their lands. Different tools helped them track this odd activity.

RADAR

Since the 1947 sightings, the U.S. military used radar to study UFOs. Radar can detect distant moving objects.

A transmitter sends out radio waves. The waves bounce off objects and return to a receiver.

The objects show up as tiny marks, or blips, on a radar screen.

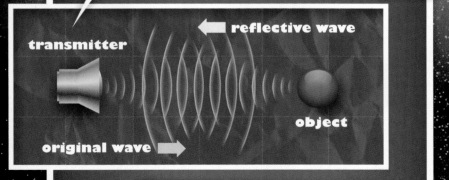

reflective wave

transmitter

object

original wave

Radar systems also create recordings of what they find. Experts can go back and study what was reported over a certain period of time.

CAMERAS ON THE SKIES

Governments have also used cameras to try to record UFOs. After many sightings near military bases in 1949, the U.S. military set up film cameras near the bases. The cameras ran 24 hours a day. They did not record anything strange.

During the 1950s, several countries set up cameras to record lights in the sky. The cameras could be left outdoors for long periods of time. They automatically switched on at night.

In 1967 Dr. Gerald R. Rothberg used the camera system to look for UFOs. These cameras could view large parts of the sky. But they couldn't take clear shots of fast-moving objects. Rothberg concluded that the system would not work well in UFO research.

Starting in 1964, the United States had ten camera systems for recording meteor showers. Scientists began examining pictures taken near reported UFO sightings. Most of the objects recorded related to normal events in space. But scientists could not say all of the objects did.

LEADING THE SEARCH

For decades, scientist J. Allen Hynek studied UFOs for the U.S. government. He offered scientific explanations for many UFO sightings. But eventually, Hynek became discouraged with government officials. He thought they were too quick to dismiss the possibility of alien life.

Hynek believed scientists should study all the possibilities for explaining UFOs. Hynek founded the Center for UFO Studies (CUFOS) in 1973.

CUFOS has a computer record of more than 100,000 UFO sightings. The reports date back more than 30 years. Today scientists at CUFOS gather reports on UFO sightings around the world. The center also publishes books and magazines about UFO studies. Some members investigate famous UFO events, such as the crash near Roswell.

CUFOS' Web site has a form people can fill out to report UFO sightings.

CLOSE ENCOUNTERS

Hynek created a system for describing close encounters with UFOs. For an encounter to be considered "close" a person must be within 200 yards (183 m) of a UFO. Hynek's system describes three kinds of close encounters.

1ST
▷ visual sighting of a UFO

2ND
▷ visual sighting of a UFO
▷ evidence that the UFO has affected the environment

3RD
▷ a sighting in which witnesses report seeing alien beings

FACT

In 1977 the movie *Close Encounters of the Third Kind* was released. The movie was about aliens contacting Earth. Hynek made a guest appearance in the movie.

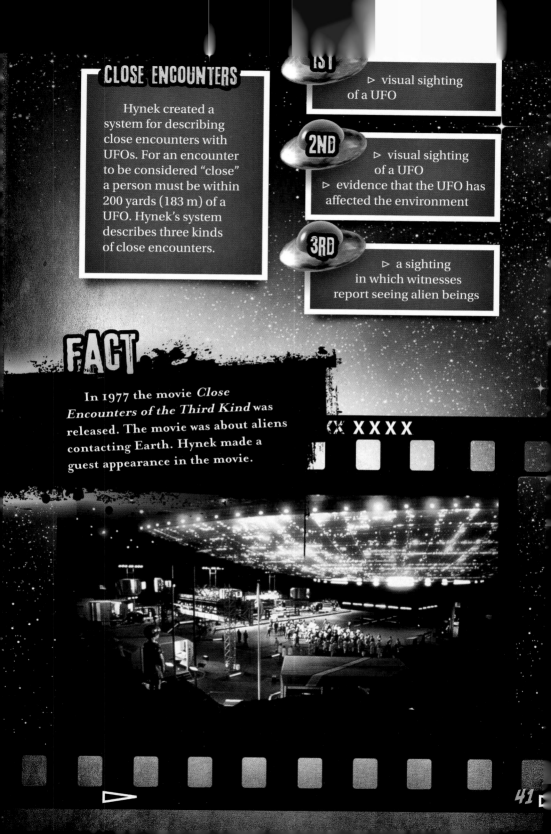

THE HESSDALEN PROJECT

Not all efforts to study UFOs are by governments. One major effort occurred in Hessdalen, Norway. In the early 1980s, mysterious lights started appearing in the sky over Hessdalen.

Sometimes witnesses reported seeing many lights over Hessdalen. Other times they saw one large **orb**. People said the lights fell to the ground, and a blue spiral of light rose up.

orb	a round light in the sky

Over the years, curious citizens set up cameras to record the Hessdalen lights. In 2000 scientists from Norway and Italy joined the project. They studied the pictures and other data. They said most of the lights were clearly natural events. But others could not be explained.

THE SEARCH IS ON

Today both governments and private groups work together to search the skies. Researchers in the United States took the first steps in the Search for Extraterrestrial Intelligence (SETI) in 1959. SETI researchers think that if aliens exist, they might have the same technology humans do. SETI telescopes scan the skies trying to pick up alien radio signals. So far, they haven't found anything that has an alien origin.

FACT

In 1961 scientist Frank Drake created an interesting mathematical formula. It predicted how many planets in our galaxy, the Milky Way, could support intelligent life. According to Drake's formula, that number is about 10,000.

THE MYSTERY REMAINS

People have studied UFOs for decades. But no definite conclusions have been reached. Astronomers say the Milky Way has about 100 billion stars similar to the sun. There is a chance that some of these stars have planets where life could form. But even if alien life exists, few scientists think they could build ships able to reach Earth.

FACT

In 2009 the U.S. government launched a spacecraft called *Kepler*. *Kepler* will travel near different stars. Special onboard sensors will search for planets that might support life.

ENDLESS POSSIBILITIES

Some scientists think certain technologies could send an aircraft over many **light years** of space. These aircraft might use magnets or the energy stored in atoms. Other scientists talk about traveling through **wormholes**. These supposed shortcuts through space would let a spacecraft cover huge distances.

Humans are not even close to building ships that could travel many light years. But some people believe aliens could be more advanced than humans.

Believers point out that people once thought traveling to the moon was impossible. These people say we can't rule out that some UFOs come from other planets. Still, most scientists reject the idea because there is no proof. Both sides continue their efforts to explain the causes of UFOs.

light year   the distance light travels in one year; one light year is 5.88 trillion miles (9.5 trillion km)

wormhole   a tunnel that creates a shortcut between two points in space that are normally very far apart; scientists are unsure whether wormholes exist

GLOSSARY

artifact (AR-tuh-fakt)—an object made by people in the past

controversy (KON-truh-vur-see)—something that people disagree about

debris (duh-BREE)—the remains of something that has been destroyed

hypnosis (hip-NOH-siss)—the process of putting someone in a trancelike state to help them remember things

illusion (i-LOO-zhuhn)—something that appears to be real but isn't

light year (LITE YEER)—the distance light travels in one year; one light year is 5.88 trillion miles (9.5 trillion km)

mirage (muh-RAHZH)—something that appears to be there but is not; mirages are often caused by light rays bending where air layers of different temperatures meet

orb (ORB)—a round light in the sky

radar (RAY-dar)—a device that uses radio waves to track the location of objects

radiation (ray-dee-AY-shuhn)—tiny particles sent out from harmful radioactive material

supernatural (soo-per-NACH-ur-uhl)—describes something that cannot be given an ordinary explanation

ufologist (yoo–FALL-uh-jist)—a person who studies and tries to explain UFOs

wormhole (WERM HOLE)—a tunnel that creates a shortcut between two points in space that are normally very far apart; scientists are unsure if wormholes exist

READ MORE

Miller, Connie Colwell. *UFOs: the Unsolved Mystery.* Mysteries of Science. Mankato, Minn.: Capstone Press, 2009.

Nobleman, Marc Tyler. *Aliens and UFOs.* Atomic. Chicago: Raintree, 2007.

Walker, Kathryn. *Mysteries of Alien Visitors and Abductions.* Unsolved! New York: Crabtree Pub. Co., 2009.

INTERNET SITES

FactHound offers a safe, fun way to find Internet sites related to this book. All of the sites on FactHound have been researched by our staff.

Here's all you do:

Visit *www.facthound.com*

Type in this code: 9781429648165

INDEX